The Battle of Atlanta

A Captivating Guide to a Battle of the Atlanta Campaign That Changed the Course of the American Civil War

© Copyright 2023 - All rights reserved.

The content contained within this book may not be reproduced, duplicated, or transmitted without direct written permission from the author or the publisher.

Under no circumstances will any blame or legal responsibility be held against the publisher, or author, for any damages, reparation, or monetary loss due to the information contained within this book, either directly or indirectly.

Legal Notice:

This book is copyright protected. It is only for personal use. You cannot amend, distribute, sell, use, quote, or paraphrase any part, or the content within this book, without the consent of the author or publisher.

Disclaimer Notice:

Please note the information contained within this document is for educational and entertainment purposes only. All effort has been executed to present accurate, up-to-date, reliable, and complete information. No warranties of any kind are declared or implied. Readers acknowledge that the author is not engaging in the rendering of legal, financial, medical, or professional advice. The content within this book has been derived from various sources. Please consult a licensed professional before attempting any techniques outlined in this book.

By reading this document, the reader agrees that under no circumstances is the author responsible for any losses, direct or indirect, that are incurred as a result of the use of the information contained within this document, including, but not limited to, errors, omissions, or inaccuracies.

Free Bonus from Captivating History (Available for a Limited time)

Hi History Lovers!

Now you have a chance to join our exclusive history list so you can get your first history ebook for free as well as discounts and a potential to get more history books for free! Simply visit the link below to join.

Captivatinghistory.com/ebook

Also, make sure to follow us on Facebook, Twitter and Youtube by searching for Captivating History.

Table of Contents

INTRODUCTION 1
CHAPTER 1 - IGNITING THE FIRES OF WAR 4
CHAPTER 2 - THE KEY PLAYERS 9
CHAPTER 3 - PRELUDE TO THE BATTLE 18
CHAPTER 4 - THE MIDNIGHT MARCH 25
CHAPTER 5 - A BLOODY BATTLE OF CRIMSON 29
CHAPTER 6 - THE CLASH CONTINUES 32
CHAPTER 7 - THE DESPERATE DASH TO CUT SUPPLY LINES 36
CHAPTER 8 - THE FALL OF ATLANTA 41
CONCLUSION 44
HERE'S ANOTHER BOOK BY CAPTIVATING HISTORY THAT
YOU MIGHT LIKE 46
FREE BONUS FROM CAPTIVATING HISTORY (AVAILABLE FOR A
LIMITED TIME) 47
REFERENCES 48

Introduction

"War is hell."

These three words encapsulate the raw brutality and unyielding suffering that accompanied the Battle of Atlanta. Ironically, Union General William Tecumseh Sherman said them. His brutal actions during the American Civil War reverberate through the annals of history because they showcase how true these words can be.

In 1864, a bloody reality descended upon the American South. What started as a fervent clash of principles transformed into an all-consuming war, with the Union Army representing the North and the Confederacy Army the South.

The flames of conflict engulfed the land, and Atlanta, Georgia, became a symbol of the Confederacy's resolve. Its capture or defense could sway the tide of the war. The Union general, known for his audacity and relentless "March to the Sea," firmly fixed his sights on the city. Although Atlanta's fate hung in the balance, Confederate General John Bell Hood fortified his defenses. He was determined to hold the city at all costs. All of this set the stage for a momentous battle as both armies converged on the war-torn area.

Our journey begins in the sweltering Georgia summer. Surrounded by the rolling hills and verdant landscapes of Atlanta, soldiers marched into history. These brave individuals hailed from all corners of the nation, donning blue and gray, united in their dedication to their respective causes. They were fathers, sons, brothers, and friends thrust into a crucible of fire and steel.

The soldiers had the type of grit that only war could summon. They braced themselves for the trials that lay ahead. Each of them endured the oppressive summer heat and thunderous cannon fire on the battlefield. They desired victory but also faced the ever-present specter of death and the longing for home.

However, the story of the Battle of Atlanta encompasses more than just the soldiers. The civilians found themselves swept in the maelstrom of war too. Men and women who called Atlanta home faced hardships that tested their resolve. The American Civil War was an encroaching danger that crept to their doorsteps and shattered their illusions of security. These civilians were forced to confront the brutal realities of conflict as the sound of artillery became a haunting lullaby.

Within Atlanta, families sought refuge and clung to fragments of normalcy amidst the chaos. Mothers consoled frightened children. Fathers braced themselves for the inevitable. Lovers clung to each other, their futures uncertain. Through their eyes, we witness the indomitable spirit that emerges when a city becomes a battleground. We share in their hopes and fears, losses and triumphs as they navigate the treacherous path between survival and despair.

The Battle of Atlanta stands as a testament to humans' capacity for both great heroism and profound tragedy. Get ready to journey into the heart of war, where echoes of the past resonate with haunting clarity. Better still, as you read this book, immerse yourself in the account by picturing yourself experiencing the events.

Imagine you're a soldier clad in the Union's blue or the Confederacy's gray. You're standing on the precipice of a battlefield. The air cracks with tension as the sun beats down mercilessly, mirroring the scorching turmoil that awaits. You can almost taste the acrid smoke that hangs heavy in the air, mingling with the stench of sweat and gunpowder. Can you hear the thunderous roar of cannons and the cries of your comrades-in-arms? Can you feel the weight of your weapon, your heart pounding in your chest, as you listen for the command to charge?

Maybe you're a woman who wants to fight as a soldier. No, you do not get a congratulatory pat on the back. Most people won't consider your becoming a soldier an honor. You don't even get the chance to enlist in the army even though you're fighting for your ideals and beliefs. Instead, you have to dress as a man, sneak out of the house, and pretend to be male.

Picture yourself as a wife watching your husband march off to battle. Anxiety grips your heart with each passing day. The silence of an empty home echoes with your worries and prayers, and you cling to memories, hoping they'll sustain you until his return. Or maybe you're a mother with the unbearable anguish of sending your young son off to war, a war he might never return from. Your heart clenches with each cannon's blast as you hope he is shielded from the horrors of battle.

Now, shift your perspective. You could be a husband bidding farewell to your beloved wife. Both of you know the uncertain fate that awaits. When your eyes meet, you see the love, fear, and longing in her. Can you sense the bittersweet ache of separation, the torment of not knowing if you'll ever hold each other again? You could be a father filled with pride and dread as you picture your son marching alongside seasoned soldiers. The weight of responsibility bears on your shoulders, and you can only hope he'll return to your embrace.

But war does not discriminate, nor does it spare the young. Imagine you're a young boy or girl peering through a cracked window as the battle rages on. Your mother tries to drag you off to the cellar, but you stay put. The world outside has transformed into a nightmarish symphony of chaos and destruction. The innocence of youth is shattered because you've witnessed the toll of war firsthand. The sight of wounded soldiers and the deafening cries of agony haunt your dreams, forever etching images of suffering onto your tender soul.

So, join me on this journey to step into the shoes of soldiers, husbands, wives, mothers, fathers, boys, and girls. Let us explore the Battle of Atlanta, not as distant spectators but as active participants in the tapestry of history.

Through the eyes of soldiers and civilians alike, we will unravel the threads of courage and desperation, tracing the contours of a battle that defined the American nation. Together, we'll discover the extraordinary stories of bravery and sacrifice, determination and resilience. We'll discover the enduring power of the human spirit in the face of unimaginable adversity. Welcome to the pages where history comes alive as we delve into a city where war became a literal hell.

Chapter 1 – Igniting the Fires of War

Let's travel back in time to the 19th century. Picture yourself standing at the crossroads of history where the fate of a nation teetered on a knife's edge. The year was 1864, and the American Civil War raged on with relentless fury.

But war doesn't begin in a day. It starts with differing opinions, opposing beliefs, unresolved conflicts, and skirmishes. The Civil War was no different. Although the nation's name was the *United* States of America, deep-seated tensions and conflicting ideologies divided it.

An Atlantan shop for auctioning and selling slaves (Negroes) in 1864.
https://commons.wikimedia.org/wiki/File:United_States_Colored_Troop_enlisted_African-American_soldier_reading_at_8_Whitehall_Street,_Atlanta_slave_auction_house,_Fall_1864-%27Auction_%26_Negro_Sales,%27_Whitehall_Street_LOC_cwpb.03351_(cropped).tif

It all began with a subject that would prove to be the powder keg of discord: slavery. The institution of slavery had become an increasingly divisive issue in America, pitting the North and South against each other like two rival siblings.

The North flourished with its factories and industrialized cities. Its burgeoning industrial economy and growing sense of moral outrage fueled a powerful anti-slavery sentiment. The South, on the other hand, depended on an agrarian economy. Slavery was an integral part of life in the Southern states. Farmers relied on enslaved labor to cultivate cotton and other cash crops, while others bought slaves to do menial jobs. The clash of these distinct economies created a deep rift that seemed insurmountable.

As sectional tensions rose, the question of states' rights versus federal authority loomed large. The Southern states staunchly defended states' rights to protect their individual liberties. They believed that each state had the autonomy to govern itself as it saw fit. Southern states wanted to be free from excessive interference from the federal government because they felt increasingly marginalized in national politics. Meanwhile, the North advocated for a more centralized authority to preserve the nation's unity.

Political factions emerged, with passionate individuals on both sides rallying behind their causes. Abraham Lincoln was elected president of the United States in 1860. This event served as a pivotal lightning rod that intensified the already simmering tensions. It set the stage for a conflict that would test the very fabric of the nation.

First, Lincoln was a Republican—a party that had little appeal to voters in the South. Almost all his votes came from the North. He won without even carrying a single Southern state. Second, he had an anti-slavery stance and a commitment to preserve the union of the states. So, he was a threat to the South's economic reliance on slavery.

To protect their interests, Southern states swiftly seceded from the Union. South Carolina took the lead, followed by six more states: Georgia, Mississippi, Alabama, Florida, Louisiana, and Texas. Four other Southern states joined them later. They united under a different flag and claimed their independence from the United States. The new nation was called the Confederate States of America.

The bombardment of Fort Sumter.
Retrieved from https://www.battlefields.org/learn/articles/problem-charleston-harbor. From Library of Congress, https://www.loc.gov/item/90711987/; No known restrictions

Finally, the die was cast for a conflict of epic proportions. The tension reached its breaking point at Fort Sumter on April 12th, 1861. This federal fort, situated in Charleston, South Carolina, became the site of the first shots fired in the Civil War. The Confederacy bombarded the military garrison at the fort, demanding its surrender, while President Lincoln sought to resupply and reinforce it. As negotiations broke down, cannons roared, and shells exploded. After thirty-four hours, the Union surrendered. No one was killed in the conflict, but this battle marked the beginning of the Civil War, the bloodiest conflict in American history.

Atlanta, Georgia, soon emerged as a critical hub of the South. It radiated both economic and military significance. This city was a symbol of the Confederacy's resilience, making it a prime target for the Union forces. What made Atlanta such a coveted prize, you may wonder? Well, let's rewind a little to the state of the bustling metropolis before the war.

Before the storm clouds of war rolled in, Atlanta was a city teeming with life and aspirations. Here, the old South mingled with progressive ambition, and the city beckoned dreamers and visionaries alike. It was the melding of old-world charm and burgeoning modernity. Victorian mansions whispered tales of Southern hospitality and charm, while factories and mills were the lifeblood of progress.

Think about the cobblestone paths of the late 1800s, the symphony of horse-drawn carriages and echoing footsteps dancing in harmony with the vibrant spirit of the city. Streets bustled with merchants, theaters echoed with laughter, and the neighborhoods hummed with the rhythm of daily life. Families, both Union and Confederate sympathizers, called this city their home, and dreams of a prosperous future resided in their hearts.

Atlanta boasted an intricate web of railroads that converged within its borders. It served as a linchpin holding the South together. It was a vital center for the Confederate Army's military operations and a critical transportation hub. Since the city was strategically located at the crossroads of several major rail lines, it connected the South to vital resources. Troops, supplies, and communication flowed through the city to support the Confederate forces on the front lines, enabling the Confederacy to wage war effectively.

But Atlanta was more than just a logistical stronghold. It was also a key supply center. It produced and warehoused vast quantities of provisions, ammunition, uniforms, and equipment, which sustained the Southern effort.

The city's communication network facilitated the dissemination of information. Its telegraph lines connected various command centers, enabling the faster transmission of orders and intelligence. Messages, orders, and other vital information from allies and spies quickly got to the Confederate Army. This web of communication allowed for swift coordination and response to Union movements. It gave the Confederacy an advantage in the ever-shifting tides of war.

The economic and industrial significance of Atlanta further solidified its importance. It had a diverse range of businesses and industries, including ironworks, foundries producing munitions, and mills churning out textiles. The city's industrial output fueled the Southern cause, providing the means to sustain the fight against the Union.

Beyond its military and economic importance, Atlanta held a symbolic weight that transcended its physical attributes. It represented the heart and soul of the Confederacy. It was a resilient bastion of Southern values, culture, determination, and defiance. Capturing the city would be a blow to the South's morale, as its defense had become a point of pride.

The city fueled the Southern war machine, making it a prime target of the Union. Its capture or defense had great importance to both sides.

Preparing to face the impending storm of Union aggression, Confederate forces bolstered Atlanta's defenses by constructing fortifications. Meanwhile, Union General William Tecumseh Sherman was unwaveringly resolved to cripple the South. Atlanta was the key to unlocking the North's ultimate victory. It was a formidable obstacle in his path.

Now that the stage had been set and the players assembled, it was only a matter of time before the Battle of Atlanta occurred. To understand the battle better, we need to look at the events that led to it and its key players.

Chapter 2 – The Key Players

The Battle of Atlanta had three prominent commanders: General William Tecumseh Sherman, General Joseph Eggleston Johnston, and General John Bell Hood. Each man had unique attributes, background, personality, and outlook on the Civil War, which shaped his plans and strategies. Let us delve into their minds as they prepared for the cataclysmic confrontation that awaited them.

General William Tecumseh Sherman.
No known restrictions; https://www.loc.gov/resource/cwpb.03379/

Born in 1820 in Ohio, General William T. Sherman's early life was marked by tragedy and hardship. His father died when he was just nine, leaving his family in financial distress. Luckily, his father's friend and neighbor, Thomas Ewing, informally adopted him. Sherman later secured a congressional appointment to the United States Military Academy at West Point. There, he cultivated his military knowledge and honed his leadership skills.

General Sherman was physically imposing. He had a sturdy and tall frame. A graying beard and receding hairline framed his face. His weathered features depicted a man hardened by the trials of war. His piercing, steely gaze held an intensity that revealed a man constantly calculating and searching for the best course of action.

Sherman had a unique blend of boldness and pragmatism. He was fiercely determined and focused. He possessed a relentless drive to achieve victory. Beneath his stern exterior lay a man of keen intellect, sharp wit, and a gift for strategy. He wasn't afraid to take risks, seize opportunities, or adapt swiftly to changing circumstances.

During the Civil War, Sherman distinguished himself at the Battle of Bull Run in 1861. He later served under General Ulysses S. Grant at Shiloh, where he was promoted to major general.

Once he understood the importance of Atlanta, the general began the Atlanta Campaign. His plan was audacious yet calculated. He wanted to outflank and outmaneuver the Confederate forces defending the city. By cutting off supply lines and weakening defenses, he planned to force the Southern army into a vulnerable position and seize control of Atlanta, ultimately securing the prize he sought.

Sherman employed the strategy of total war to achieve his aim. This concept involved uncompromising aggression toward the enemy's armies and civilian populations. He believed in striking at the heart of the Confederate war effort by targeting military installations and civilian infrastructure and resources. He planned to destroy the economic resources of the Southern population, break their will, and cripple their capacity to continue the fight. It was a brutal but what he believed necessary approach to achieving a swift Union victory.

General Joseph Eggleston Johnston.
https://commons.wikimedia.org/wiki/File:Joseph_Johnston.jpg

Initially opposing Sherman in the Atlanta Campaign was General Joseph E. Johnston. He was born in 1807 to a prominent military family in Virginia. Johnston also attended the Military Academy at West Point. He demonstrated his aptitude for military studies and then served in the Mexican-American War, where he earned accolades for bravery and leadership.

General Johnston was a respected military commander with a dignified appearance that commanded attention and exuded an air of confidence. He had a neatly trimmed beard and a lean and athletic frame that belied his years. Johnston was a master of defensive warfare. He was well known for his meticulous planning and keen sense of military tactics. He employed caution, intellect, and acumen in battle. He was calm and composed under pressure. The general possessed a quiet resolve that earned him the respect and admiration of his troops.

Johnston's approach to the war contrasted starkly with Sherman's aggressive mindset. He understood that the South had limited manpower and resources. So, he advocated attrition rather than attack.

The Confederate general aimed to protect Atlanta with carefully constructed defensive lines. He believed in preserving his forces by avoiding direct confrontations unless conditions were favorable. Johnston sought to wear down the Union Army through guerilla tactics and defensive maneuvers.

His ultimate goal was to force Sherman into a costly and protracted siege. This would weaken the Union's resolve, encouraging them to make mistakes. The Southern army would then exploit the enemy's weaknesses and win.

However, Johnston's cautious approach occasionally brought him into conflict with Confederate President Jefferson Davis and other leaders who sought more aggressive action. Johnston's tendency to retreat and avoid decisive battles led to strained relationships. It also resulted in occasional reassignments during the war. That was what happened during the Atlanta Campaign, just before the Battle of Atlanta. Johnston was reassigned because his battle tactics were too defensive.

Despite these challenges, the general remained highly respected among his fellow officers. His reputation as a skilled strategist, commitment to his soldiers' well-being, and compassionate leadership endeared him to his troops, who affectionately called him "Uncle Joe."

General John Bell Hood.
https://commons.wikimedia.org/wiki/File:Lt._Gen._John_B._Hood.jpg

General John Bell Hood took over command of the Confederate Army of Tennessee from General Johnston. Hood was born in 1831 in Kentucky to a physician. He graduated from the United States Military Academy at twenty-two and joined the Confederate Army during the Civil War.

Possessing a sturdy build, prominent chin, and strong jawline, Hood had a rugged appearance that contributed to his commanding presence. He was a courageous risk-taker known for his audacity and bravery on the battlefield. He exhibited a strong sense of duty and loyalty to the Confederate cause.

Hood willingly partook in the dangers his troops faced by leading them from the front lines. He ended up sustaining injuries before the Battle of Atlanta. His left arm got wounded at Gettysburg, rendering the arm unusable. The next month, his leg was severely wounded in the Battle of Chickamauga, which led to amputating it four inches below the hip. Hood then had to rely on a manservant to help with daily tasks and crutches for movement.

Yet, even in the face of overwhelming odds, the general fought actively to defend the South. And it paid off. He was one of the most rapidly promoted officers in the Confederate Army.

Hood's leadership style was marked by his offensive-minded approach. He sought decisive victories on the battlefield by favoring direct assaults over cautious defensive strategies. He believed that taking the fight to the Union forces would enable his army to give them a decisive blow, which could weaken Northern resolve and pave the way for Confederate success. While he demonstrated tactical skill, his aggressive strategies often came at a high cost. However, his style was in line with what the Confederate president and leaders favored.

As a proud and determined commander, Hood resolved to hold onto Atlanta at all costs. He intended to rely on the city's fortifications. Then, he would engage in an offensive battle by drawing out the Union Army, attacking them, and inflicting heavy casualties. The general hoped to exploit the rugged terrain. If his army could wear down the Northern forces, he would outlast Sherman's advance and maintain control of Atlanta.

It was a risky gambit, but Hood was solely focused on the defense of Atlanta. He was willing to stake everything in his quest for victory, even if it meant sacrificing his own troops.

These three generals were instrumental in the Atlanta Campaign, especially William Sherman and John Hood, who fought against each other. Other key players were the Union and Confederate soldiers.

A variety of things pushed the Union soldiers to take up arms. Many of them went to war out of duty and patriotism. They believed it was their responsibility to defend the Union. These men saw the Confederate cause as a threat to the very idea of the Union. They also saw the battle as an opportunity to end slavery and create a more just society. Lincoln's Emancipation Proclamation allowed African Americans to enlist in the Union Army.

But it wasn't just big ideas that motivated these soldiers. Many fought to protect their homes. They didn't want Confederate forces to invade their communities, and they were willing to risk everything to keep their families safe.

Others enlisted for the promise of a regular paycheck. They hoped to escape the hardships of civilian life by earning money in the army. As soldiers, they would secure a stable income and provide for their families.

On the Confederate side, the motivations were slightly different but no less powerful. The soldiers saw the Union invasion as a threat to their property and the traditions they held dear, and they wanted to protect their families, land, and communities. To them, the battle was a pivotal moment in their struggle against Northern aggression.

Southern loyalty and patriotism were powerful driving forces for Confederate soldiers. Their allegiance to the South influenced their actions on the battlefield. A good example of such a soldier is Samuel Rush Watkins. He served in Company H in the Tennessee infantry regiment during the Atlanta Campaign. Watkins had a deep attachment to his homeland and a sense of duty to defend it against the North or the Yankees.

For some Confederate soldiers, the defense of slavery was a key motivation. They believed in preserving the institution of slavery because it was integral to their economic prowess.

Others stood by honor and duty. They were guided by principles of chivalry, courage, and loyalty and saw themselves as guardians of Southern heritage. They fought with unwavering determination. Surrender or retreat wasn't an option for them.

As soldiers from both sides fought during the Atlanta Campaign, they were driven by duty, patriotism, family, and deeply held convictions. Their motivations were constantly tested on the battlefield.

Besides the soldiers and famous battle heroes of Atlanta, there were unsung heroes who must be mentioned.

Within the city, people and institutions emerged as towers of support. As far back as 1862, hotels and municipal buildings became makeshift hospitals. Even the Atlanta Medical College suspended its classes to tend to wounded soldiers. A sprawling hospital complex was built on the fairgrounds by the Georgia Railroad. It provided aid to the countless casualties of war and helped relieve the already overcrowded hospitals.

Businesses like the Atlanta Rolling Mill were also key players. The mill was one of two in the South that could produce railroad rails, and it shifted its focus during the Civil War. Once re-rolling old rails, it now churned out iron sheets for Confederate ships, iron rails for the railroads, and cannons for the battlefields. It was a symbol of Southern industry and resilience. The mill was bought out and renamed the Confederate Rolling Mill in 1863.

Unfortunately, Georgia was wrought with problems. The Civil War's relentless march led to food shortages, particularly for yeoman or non-slaveholding farmers' families. Riots and looting erupted, as people, driven by the hunger gnawing in their stomachs and the desire to provide for their families, saw no other option for survival. Some women in Atlanta faced the agonizing decision to stay and endure the horrors of war or flee to safety. They took their children and journeyed away from the turmoil.

But in that same Atlanta, other women emerged as pillars of strength. The elite white women used their influence to encourage enlistment into the army. They appealed to the men's sense of masculinity and honor to inspire them to fight for the Confederacy.

While their husbands and sons ventured off to the battlefields, Atlanta's women took charge of their homes. Women of all classes took on roles that had been previously denied to them and became the backbone of the family. They became the managers of family farms, homes, plantations, and businesses. Working-class women found jobs in factories and arsenals. However, these opportunities were often limited to white women.

Other women helped their struggling neighbors by creating fundraising groups to support them. They formed aid societies to craft essentials for soldiers, which included socks, shirts, gloves, bandages, and blankets.

However, their contributions extended far beyond the realm of helping soldiers or families. Brave women operated as spies and scouts who gathered intelligence. Despite the constant threat of discovery, they moved past enemy lines and then conveyed crucial information about troop movements, supplies, and strategies. In doing so, they exhibited a kind of courage that challenged the norms of their time.

Some took their commitment even further. They disguised themselves as men and enlisted in the Union or Confederate army and donned the uniforms of soldiers. These women embraced the call of duty with a fervor that defied societal norms. They marched into battle, shouldered rifles, and shared the same dangers as their male counterparts.

Some females worked as nurses and volunteers in hospitals. A sixteen-year-old girl named Augusta "Gussie" King Clayton volunteered in a military hospital. In these hospitals, countless lives hung in the balance. Gussie provided a ray of hope by caring for wounded soldiers, nursing the sick, reading to the wounded, offering words of comfort, and writing letters to their loved ones. She fell victim to typhoid, a fatal disease during the Civil War. When Sherman's army arrived at the outskirts of Atlanta, Gussie was fighting for her life.

African Americans were not left out. Born into a world that had enslaved them for generations, all they knew was the bitter taste of oppression. But on January 1st, 1863, President Abraham Lincoln issued the Emancipation Proclamation that freed all slaves living in the Confederate States.

This decree was a beacon of hope for African Americans in the South. To them, the war was no longer just a fight between the North and South but a catalyst for liberation. It was a war for their very humanity, a battle to break the chains of bondage that had bound them for so long. Now, they could fight for the right to be treated as equals. Many African American men eagerly joined the Union Army, forming regiments known as the United States Colored Troops (USCT).

Unfortunately, General Sherman did not let USCT soldiers fight in his ranks. His decision did not deter some African Americans. They decided to become teamsters, general laborers, and cooks for the Union Army. At least four hundred African American cooks actively worked on the war front during the Battle of Atlanta as stretcher-bearers.

All these men and women played an active role in the Battle of Atlanta. While some of them were at the battlefront, others helped with the smooth running of operations and the well-being of soldiers during the war. Some others were on the home front, contributing in whatever way they could.

Chapter 3 – Prelude to the Battle

The sweltering summer of 1864 set the backdrop for the Battle of Atlanta. But before the clash of arms commenced, a series of events shaped the course of the conflict.

In May 1864, the Atlanta Campaign was born. General Sherman gathered his forces—the Union Army of the Cumberland, Army of the Tennessee, and Army of the Ohio—and began the relentless advance toward Atlanta. He was on a mission to seize control of the city.

The air was thick with anticipation as the Union soldiers pressed forward, their hearts filled with a thirst for victory. Their boots stirred up clouds of dust that clung to their uniform and coated their weary bodies. Sweat trickled down their faces, merging with the dirt and leaving salty trails on their skin. The scent of dirt and sweat mingled together, creating a distinctive aroma that permeated the air, a testament to the physical toll the soldiers endured.

The men trudged through heat and torrential downpours, their bodies weary, their spirits tested. They endured the sting of insect bites and the discomfort of damp uniforms. With each step, they felt the harsh terrain beneath their worn-out boots. The uneven ground, littered with rocks and tree roots, challenged their balance.

Yet, they pressed on, their minds aflame with the desire to see this campaign through. The determination to seize Atlanta and bring an end to the Confederacy's grip on the region fueled their spirits. From May to July, they fought battles along the way, such as the Battle of Resaca and the Battle of Kennesaw Mountain. In each battle, Union forces clashed with Confederate defenders.

General Sherman employed flanking strategies to outmaneuver General Johnston's defensive positions. He used swift strikes to keep the Southern forces off balance. His army launched a series of frontal assaults but faced fierce resistance. The Northern forces continued their flanking maneuvers, forcing the Confederates to retreat repeatedly. However, Sherman's path wasn't without its trials. As the campaign wore on, he faced setbacks and challenges that tested his mettle.

The Confederate Army of Tennessee, under the command of General Joseph Johnston, faced the daunting task of repelling the Union advance. Johnston recognized the numerical advantage, tenacity, and resourcefulness of his adversary. So, he refused to engage in a direct confrontation.

In an attempt to delay the Union Army's progress, he combined defensive tactics with strategic retreats. The formidable terrain and natural landscape barriers of Georgia served as valuable assets in the South's defense. Johnston used defensive warfare to buy time while waiting for the opportune moment to strike a decisive blow.

These were battles of wit as the two generals sought to outmaneuver each other, each vying for the upper hand. The campaign stretched on, the tension building with each passing day.

Confederate fortifications at Atlanta.
No known restrictions; https://www.loc.gov/item/2012646711/

Meanwhile, the Southern army had been building fortifications around Atlanta for more than a year. They intensified their efforts earlier in the summer when they heard that Sherman's forces had left Chattanooga and were marching toward Atlanta.

The Southern forces embarked on a feverish effort to transform the city into a fortress. The Confederate soldiers made slaves toil tirelessly as they raced against time to fortify their position for the inevitable battle. The civilians could hear the sound of hammers and shovels echo through the streets as men dug trenches and erected earthworks. The enslaved laborers' hands grew calloused and blistered, their muscles aching.

By July 1864, the landscape around Atlanta had transformed into a network of trenches and fortifications. Two concentric rings of fortifications arose from the Georgia soil. The inner ring was the defensive bulwarks. Stern-faced soldiers armed with glinting musket barrels stood inside the ring. They were always alert, their eyes fixed on the horizon where the Union forces approached.

The outer ring was a giant maze, a labyrinth of earthen palisades and winding trenches that snaked their way around Atlanta's outskirts. This was a cunning device intended to slow the relentless advance of the Union troops. It would serve as a barrier between the Confederates and the Union onslaught.

The Southern army stored ammunition, food, and other essential provisions in several places in the city. Artillery became the heartbeat of their defense. They handpicked cannon placements to provide maximum coverage and firepower. The soldiers positioned their cannons on high ground, allowing them to rain devastating fire on the Northern troops as they advanced. These strategically placed artillery pieces formed a formidable barrier.

However, Confederate President Jefferson Davis was dissatisfied with General Johnston's performance. Despite Johnston's cautious approach, Sherman's forces gained ground and pressed southward toward Atlanta.

Davis and other high-ranking officials favored aggressive strategies and believed Johnston wasn't doing enough to defend Atlanta. Prior to his command in Atlanta, the general had lost key battles, including the Peninsula Campaign and the defense of Richmond. His past record in battle eroded confidence in his leadership abilities. Besides, the Confederates had lost important strongholds, such as Chattanooga and

Vicksburg. The Confederate government faced mounting pressure to defend Atlanta, a vital transportation and industrial center for the Confederacy.

Wagon train leaving Atlanta in 1864.
https://en.m.wikipedia.org/wiki/File:LastTrainAtlantaDepot1864crop1.jpg

As the Union forces closed in on the city, Johnston ordered the evacuation of the military hospitals and ammunition machinery in Atlanta. Residents were distressed about the approaching Northern troops, and some fled. The urgency to defend Atlanta intensified.

There was a growing belief that Confederate forces needed a change in command to bolster Atlanta's defenses and mount a more aggressive resistance. The government felt that a more offensive-minded commander would prevent the loss of the city by confronting the Northern forces head-on. A week later, President Davis relieved Johnston of his command. Davis replaced him with General John Bell Hood, a lieutenant general and corps commander in the Army of Tennessee.

Hood, known for his more assertive approach, was seen as a better fit for defending Atlanta. He assumed his new position on July 17th, 1864, and was made a full general with temporary rank the next day.

By this time, the Union Army was five miles away from the outskirts of Atlanta. Once Hood took over the reins of the Confederate Army of Tennessee, he sought to shift the strategy of his forces from defense to offense. He hoped to take the fight directly to Sherman and inflict a crippling blow that would drive the Union Army from the gates of Atlanta.

While Sherman's forces were advancing toward the city from other directions, the Army of the Cumberland, commanded by General George H. Thomas, was crossing Peach Tree Creek. This was one of the three armies that had combined to form the Union forces under Sherman. General Hood saw this event as an opportunity to devastate the enemy's forces. His aim was to isolate and destroy the Cumberland troops before the other two armies could render assistance. On the night of July 19th, Hood met with his generals and planned an attack on Thomas's army.

The stage was set for a decisive confrontation. The Union's disposition on that fateful night seemed to beckon the Confederates to attack. The plan, in theory, was sound. Thomas's troops were spread thin and were vulnerable in their unfortified positions while crossing Peach Tree Creek. They were also miles away from other Union troops.

But as the first rays of dawn bathed the battlefield on July 20th, General Hood's grand design began to unravel. The Battle of Peach Tree Creek unfolded with a series of missteps that sent his plan spiraling into disarray. Thomas's forces had made staggering progress under cover of night, forcing the Confederate right flank to reposition itself, which wasted precious time. Within that period, the Union Army boldly established its defensive positions.

The sun hung high in the sky, casting a golden glow upon the battlefield. But time wasn't on Hood's side. It wasn't until 3:30 p.m. that the South's right flank launched an attack. The crack of musket fire filled the air as Union soldiers unleashed a storm of lead upon the advancing Confederates. The Southerners, unfettered, pressed on, launching relentless charges.

For a short while, the Confederate attackers threatened to envelop the Union lines. In a brief glimmer of hope, the Southerners temporarily overran a portion of the Northern lines. But their triumph was short-lived. The Union Army regrouped and pushed back with a vengeance.

They swiftly adjusted their defenses, holding the line with unwavering resolve. Their counterattack forced the Confederate troops to retreat.

As the sun set, the Confederates recognized the futility of further engagement and withdrew. The Battle of Peach Tree Creek had come to a bitter end. Hood's plan had crumbled beneath the weight of fierce Union resistance. The once-promising attack had faltered, leaving behind the memory of failure.

The battlefield lay cloaked in an eerie stillness, broken only by the soft moans of the wounded and the rumble of retreating Confederate soldiers. The dust and smoke, once stirred by the relentless clashes, now hung in the air like a somber shroud. The sun set on a landscape marred by the carnage of battle, casting long shadows over the fallen. Hood's aspiration of victory had been dashed. The brave souls who fought under his command were left to grapple with the bitter taste of defeat.

The casualty count told a grim tale. Around 2,500 Confederate lives were lost, while the Union forces mourned approximately 1,750 comrades. The Battle of Peach Tree Creek drew blood on both sides. It was a clash where dreams of victory collided with the harsh realities of war. It foreshadowed the intensity of the conflict yet to come.

The sights and sounds of the battlefield, the cries of bravery, and the stench of gunpowder were etched into the memories of the soldiers involved. For Hood, it was a bitter setback and a blow that tested his resolve.

On the other hand, the Battle of Peach Tree Creek further strengthened Sherman's position. Although the Union forces achieved a tactical victory, it wasn't without cost.

As the Union forces drew close to Atlanta, a sense of anticipation filled the air. The city loomed on the horizon, a beacon of Confederate pride and defiance. The Northern soldiers could almost taste victory, a bittersweet taste on their tongue, knowing that it would come at a great cost.

The once-thriving Atlanta, known as the gate city of the South, now lay under the shadow of impending doom. The lives of civilians far from the front lines weren't less harrowing. From the porch of her home, nine-year-old Carrie Berry could hear the war. Quiet days had become increasingly rare. Instead, they were replaced with the distant rumble of cannons and the sharp crack of muskets. Carrie dreaded the shells the most. They broke through structures, causing many deaths.

There was only one sanctuary when the shells descended—the cellar. The walls were a bit thicker, the air a tad more breathable. It offered a fragile shield against the onslaught. Carrie and her family huddled together in there when the shells descended, but that didn't stop them from experiencing the destruction the shells brought. One busted under their dining room. Another passed through the smokehouse and fell through the top of their house. Luckily, they were in Carrie's aunt's home when the shells damaged their house.

This was the grim reality for Atlantan civilians. Streets that once bustled with commerce were now filled with danger and hushed whispers. The state of Atlanta mirrored the state of its people. It was a city teetering between hope and despair. The tension was palpable. In this raging war, the fate of Atlanta hung precariously in the balance.

Chapter 4 – The Midnight March

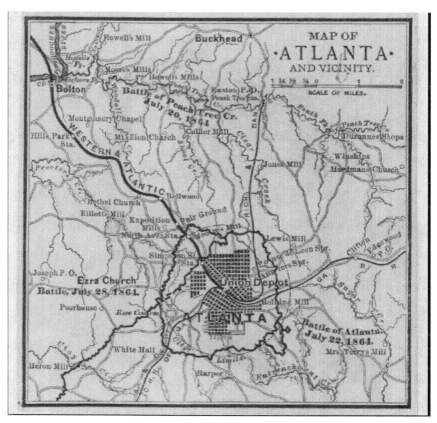

Map of Atlanta during the Civil War.
https://commons.wikimedia.org/wiki/File:Map_of_Atlanta_and_vicinity,_(July_1864),_LOC_994 47304.jpg

After the Union victory at the Battle of Peach Tree Creek, General Sherman shifted his focus to the Army of Tennessee commanded by Major General James B. McPherson. He needed a vantage point for his soldiers, somewhere he and his commander could easily observe Atlanta and fight with a higher chance of victory. The most logical place to set up camp was Bald Hill, which overlooked the Georgia Railroad junction connecting Atlanta to Decatur.

General Hood, anticipating the move, sent his troops to Bald Hill. About two thousand cavalrymen from his army got there first and occupied the hill. The Union troops descended on them like a tempest, attacking at mid-morning on July 21st. The Confederates fought fiercely, but they were forced to withdraw to a nearby wooded tract, leaving Bald Hill to the Federals.

Hood did not give up, though. He was resolute and determined to win Bald Hill back, so he drew up plans for a daring maneuver. He arranged for some soldiers to guard Atlanta from the inner ring fortification, then ordered the rest of his troops to embark on a long night march, aiming to come in behind the Northern forces. This would disrupt the Union position and turn the tide of the battle.

However, in the fog of war, the Southern general had overlooked a crucial detail. His plan hinged on his commander withdrawing his men from battle, a task easier said than done. Hours passed, and the night grew darker before the Confederate forces assembled and began their fifteen-mile march. The Confederate skirmishers held their positions to mask the withdrawal of the seventeen thousand to eighteen thousand soldiers.

There must have been a seemingly endless column of weary men, their boots shuffling on the dusty road. Remember, they had fought the Battle of Peach Tree Creek on July 20th and fought off the attacking Union forces the next day. Yet, that same night, they were trekking to attack the Northern army's left flank. Maybe the moon was out that night, and the twinkling stars were the Confederate soldiers' guiding light. Or it could have been a night of thick darkness. The path ahead would have been illuminated by the occasional flicker of a lantern casting eerie shadows on the marching brigade of soldiers.

The night was filled with hushed footfalls and jingling equipment. The rifles' carry-on straps pressed into the soldiers' shoulders. The ever-present humidity clung to their skin. The soldiers' gray uniforms were stained with sweat and dust from the road. With each step in the dense, shadowy woods, the chill of the night crept into their uniforms.

These soldiers couldn't stop their trek to even make a campfire for the night because they had an audacious goal in their minds. They would attack the weakened rear of the Union Army's left flank in the morning and then destroy Sherman's supply train. But by the time morning light crept over the battlefield, Hood's troops had barely reached the halfway point of their journey.

Sherman had his own gambit unfolding. He had moved his headquarters to Augustus Hurt House, Decatur, which was strategically located on a nearby hill just two miles east of Atlanta. He surveyed the city's fortifications from the high ground. It was a commander's view of the battlefield, which could be likened to a chessboard.

Sherman believed that conquering Atlanta would hasten the end of the Civil War, and he had to do everything possible to take the city from the Confederates and annihilate its power. So, he sent the Army of the Tennessee to destroy the Georgia Railroad that came into Atlanta from the east.

As dawn's first light illuminated the sky, Sherman received good news: Hood's forces had vacated the outer ring of the city's defenses. Not wanting to waste such an awesome opportunity, the general ordered his troops to pursue them. He was about to send an infantry corps away from his left flank when McPherson cautioned him that it would make the army vulnerable. Sherman listened to McPherson's counsel and rescinded his orders, a decision that would prove to be the salvation of the Union forces.

McPherson arranged his thirty-five thousand troops in a sprawling L-shaped formation. The vertical section faced north-south, while the horizontal section extended east-west. Bald Hill, later to be named Leggett's Hill, was fortified with cannons and a sentinel overlooking the battlefield.

Unfortunately for Hood, fate had other designs for him and his audacious attack strategy. His army was hampered by the harsh terrain. He also didn't know the full extent of McPherson's formidable line. When the general's infantry took their positions, they were six agonizing hours behind schedule, and McPherson was ready for him.

The Battle of Atlanta was about to begin. The night march had brought the Confederate forces to a moment that would define their lives and the course of history. Although the troops met a different situation from what they expected, they stood ready to face whatever the day would bring.

Chapter 5 – A Bloody Battle of Crimson

July 22nd, 1864, dawned with a palpable sense of anticipation. General Hood had strategized for the Battle of Atlanta by planning to catch the weakened rear of the Union troops unawares. But as the day unfolded, it became clear that his attack faced insurmountable challenges.

The rugged terrain, which had been an advantage during General Johnston's command, slowed the Southern army's advance to a crawl. So, the attack Hood planned as a dawn assault was delayed until the afternoon.

Sweat-soaked uniforms clung to the skin of the Southern soldiers. The Confederates were weary from their nightlong journey by the time they arrived, but they found themselves facing well-entrenched Northern troops. The Confederates were directly in front of fortified Union soldiers. McPherson had also extended his line eastward. The front lines were etched along Flat Shoals Road and Moreland Avenue, stretching from the vibrant East Atlanta Village to where the Inman Park MARTA station stands today.

The over seventy-five thousand soldiers wearing the Northern blue and Confederate gray stood before each other, and both sides began to battle. Commanders shouted orders, and each army moved as a unit. While the heat from the sun pressed down upon them, the soldiers focused on winning the battle.

General Hood watched the battle from the home of Atlanta Mayor James Calhoun. The house, which was at the highest point of where Historic Oakland Cemetery stands today, provided a commanding view of the clash. Sherman watched the battle from his vantage point, which was opposite Hood's location. His mind calculated every move as the soldiers fought.

For a brief moment, Hood's troops breached the Union lines. The Confederate soldiers exploited the newly gained position by attacking the Yankees with a visceral intensity. McPherson noticed that there was a chink in that position and galloped toward it to inspect the ongoing battle. Hood's infantry noticed him and shot him. He died a short while later.

Despite McPherson's death, the Union soldiers' spirits were not broken. They held their positions atop Bald Hill. They drove the Confederates back, and the South's newly gained position quickly slipped through the Southern troops' grasp.

As the sun beat down mercilessly, the cacophony of war prevailed. The deafening roar of cannon and musket fire drowned out natural sounds in the environment. The acrid stench of spent gunpowder mingled with the heavy, sweat-soaked air. Union and Confederate forces clashed with primal fury. Wave after wave of Hood's troops surged up the hill, their battle cries loud and unrelenting. The Northern soldiers met the onslaught with unwavering resolve. Despite the ferocity and relentless push of the South's infantry, they held the line.

By late afternoon, the sun cast long shadows on the battlefield. The Confederates exploited another weak spot in the Union lines. They attacked a vulnerable spot at an exposed railroad to the north. Aware of their precarious position, Sherman's forces retreated eastward.

However, a Union commander led a valiant counterattack, preventing reinforcements from reaching Hood's soldiers. The Confederate forces were repulsed again and again, their ranks thinning with every futile charge.

As the day wore on, the nice green fields turned a gruesome shade of crimson with the blood of the fallen. The bodies of Southern and Northern soldiers lay in macabre piles, their forms twisted and mingled by the merciless hail of bullets. It was a tableau of death and destruction. It was a chilling sight, even for those who had seen the horrors of war before. The battle, which lasted around nine hours, exacted a heavy toll on both sides. The Confederate troops were forced to retreat when they could no longer bear any more losses.

When the dust and smoke finally settled, the full extent of the battle's devastation became painfully clear. The South suffered approximately 5,500 causalities (either dead, wounded, captured, or missing). The Union forces also paid a steep price for victory, with about 3,700 casualties. The cost of this battle was dire. Two major generals, James Birdseye McPherson of the Union Army and William Henry Talbot Walker of the Confederate Army, never left the battlefield alive. Their loss was keenly felt by both armies.

But the toll extended beyond the battlefield. On that same fateful day, Augusta "Gussie" King Clayton, who had been volunteering in Atlanta's military hospitals, died from typhoid. Her passing was a heart-wrenching loss deeply felt by her family and the city. With shells still raining upon Atlanta, Gussie's family couldn't hold a proper funeral for her. Instead, they laid her to rest in the family garden. It was a somber and makeshift farewell to a young life cut short too soon.

To Sherman, the battle had not reached a decisive conclusion. Although Atlanta wasn't an easy prize, it was a much-needed one. The Civil War, which had lasted for more than three years by this point, had steadily eroded President Abraham Lincoln's popularity. There was a looming election, and the electorate was losing hope in Lincoln. The president had to secure Atlanta, a symbol of Southern defiance, to tip the scales in his favor. And it was Sherman's job to deliver it to him.

While the Confederates had done a great job of fortifying Atlanta, the fortification was too close to the city center. It left the city vulnerable to the maximum range of the Union cannons. After the battle, Sherman gazed at the earthworks and trenches. He realized that raining cannon fire on Atlanta was necessary for a Union victory. So, he laid siege and bombarded the city with artillery.

The Battle of Atlanta was the second time in a mere three days that General Hood's efforts to dislodge the Union grip on Atlanta had failed. His relentless drive to reclaim Bald Hill (or Leggett's Hill) had met resolute opposition as the Yankees clung tenaciously to their prize. The Confederates' already-outnumbered army paid dearly for the battle.

The victory of the Northern soldiers on July 22nd, 1864, marked a turning point in the war. It didn't lead to the Confederates giving up the city, but it set the stage for Atlanta's eventual fall.

Chapter 6 – The Clash Continues

After a long battle, what do soldiers do? They rest. If they have won, they jubilate and celebrate. If they are losing or expect another battle after winning, they rest and re-strategize to anticipate the enemy's next move.

And that was what the Union and Confederate armies did. The Northern Army of the Tennessee remained at Bald Hill and placed some soldiers at the perimeter to guard it. The Southerners retreated back to the Atlanta fortifications outside the city. In each army, soldiers regrouped to ensure that they were accounted for and that their chain of command remained intact. Units that suffered heavy casualties were reorganized.

Meanwhile, medics and medical personnel treated wounded soldiers, prioritizing the critically injured. They transported soldiers who required extensive medical care to hospitals or medical facilities and treated the rest on the battlefield.

The soldiers gathered information from intelligence personnel and captured enemy soldiers, then sent reports to their respective generals. Some recovered, while others identified the dead or wounded. Some focused on checking their ammunition and supply needs. Food, water, and other supplies were distributed to replenish the fighting men's resources while they inspected and conducted maintenance on their weapons and equipment.

Since McPherson had passed away, General Sherman put the Union Army of the Tennessee under the command of Major General Oliver

O. Howard. Sherman decided to prevent supplies from entering Atlanta. He sent the Army of the Ohio to the east edge of the city and the Army of the Cumberland to the north. Then, he maneuvered the Army of the Tennessee into position on the city's western flank. The mission was clear: cut the Atlanta and West Point Railroad, a transport route that brought in supplies from East Point, Georgia, into Atlanta. This strategy would strangle the life out of the city and force the Confederates to evacuate. Howard's troops set out on the morning of July 27th.

But General Hood had held a vise-like grip on Atlanta. Resolute in his defense, his indomitable spirit refused to yield. He aimed to relieve the mounting pressure on the city and disrupt Sherman's siege. It wasn't surprising that the Confederate cavalry detected the Northern troops' advance with precision. At 4.15 a.m., a few hours after Howard's departure, a warning reached Hood's headquarters. The message said, "Indications are that the enemy will attack our left."

Howard's troops, undeterred by the predawn hour, kept marching until they extended the Union line to the railroad. By nightfall, the Confederate cavalry's predictions had manifested into reality. Howard's men shifted Sherman's right flank nearly two miles to the south, positioning themselves due west of Atlanta. By July 28th, the soldiers had dug into the earth to place artillery as fortifications.

Determined to thwart the Union plan, Hood dispatched two formidable corps to intercept the Federal threat. They were to march westward along Lick Skillet Road, seize the crossroads near Ezra Church, and entrench facing north. Ezra Church was a modest yet strategically placed Methodist church located about five miles southwest of downtown Atlanta.

Hood wanted his men to launch a surprise attack on the enemy. Catching them unprepared could spell victory for the South and alter the course of the Atlanta Campaign. Nevertheless, maintaining the element of surprise in the fluid dynamics of a Civil War campaign was exceedingly challenging.

Some Union soldiers at the Battle of Ezra Church.
https://commons.wikimedia.org/wiki/File:BattleOfEzraChurchHarpersWeekly.jpg

Howard, who had been Hood's classmate at West Point, had anticipated the attack. He had placed one of his corps in the Confederate Army's path. They piled rails and logs to fashion makeshift breastworks and earthworks before the Southern army arrived. The Union infantry now held Ezra Church and Lick Skillet junction, rendering General Hood's plan obsolete.

The Confederate corps commander, Lieutenant General Stephen D. Lee, impulsively decided to attack head-on. He believed they could seize the crossroads before the Yankees could become entrenched. The clash that followed was a chaotic symphony of musket fire, the woods echoing with the cries of men locked in desperate combat.

The Union infantry, ensconced behind their makeshift defenses, unleashed a torrent of bullets. Simultaneously, Union artillery units unleashed a devastating crossfire upon the advancing Southern troops. The Confederate division, which was attempting a frontal assault, bore the brunt of the storm. It was a devastating charge met with withering fire. So, the Confederates were compelled to fall back, leaving the field strewn with their fallen comrades. Undaunted by the casualties, they called upon reinforcements.

In the midst of the tumult, the Northern army clung tenaciously to Ezra Church. Desperate to enforce their defenses, the men even dismantled the pews within the church to bolster the barricades.

Another division joined the Southerners, and their attacks began to unravel. Their assaults became uncoordinated and disjointed as each unit arrived piecemeal on the battlefield. The result was more carnage, with musket volleys felling Confederates by the hundreds.

Hours later, the day drew to a close, but the conflict raged on. The Battle of Ezra Church spiraled into a maelstrom of violence. The fighting was brutal, often dissolving into close-quarters combat. Southern soldiers confronted overwhelming odds as they tried to breach the Union lines. They launched multiple assaults, but each was met with fierce resistance from the Northerners. Despite their valor and determination, the Confederate attackers struggled to make headway against the Union defenders.

As day turned into night, the intensity of the battle gradually waned. Skirmishes continued until cover of darkness allowed the Confederates to slip away, leaving the place to the Union forces.

When the dust finally settled, the fields and woods surrounding Ezra Church were strewn with the lifeless and wounded. Both Union and Confederate forces retrieved their fallen and cared for the injured. Field hospitals bustled with activity as medical personnel worked tirelessly to save lives and offer solace to the suffering.

The Battle of Ezra Church concluded with a Union victory. The South suffered grievous losses, with estimates exceeding between 2,800 and 3,000 casualties. In contrast, the Northern forces recorded fewer than 650 men lost. Howard's defenses, though resolute, had not cut the rail tracks. While a tactical defeat for the Confederates, the battle prevented the Union troops from reaching the coveted rail line. Lee and his corps marched on and guarded the railroad.

The battle was over, yet the war raged on. The struggle for Atlanta, with its symbolic and strategic significance, remained far from decided. The South had once again defended its ground, but the city's ultimate fate still hung precariously in the balance.

Chapter 7 – The Desperate Dash to Cut Supply Lines

All through this time, Carrie Berry still lived in Atlanta. But all she could think about was the shelling and the muskets shooting. Whenever the shelling became too much, she and her family hid in their small cellar. Carrie's ten-year birthday was on August 3rd, but she couldn't celebrate with a cake because times were too hard. She only had one birthday wish—let there be peace in the land on her next birthday so she could have a nice dinner.

Meanwhile, General Sherman was still trying to cut off supplies from Atlanta and the Confederates. While his artillery bombarded Atlanta, he decided to keep trying to cut off the Macon and Western Railroad, which was between Atlanta and East Point. By July 31st, Howard was almost at the railroad. The general sent the Army of the Ohio to take up a position at Howard's right. The Army of the Ohio marched out on August 2nd. They settled into their new position two miles away from the rail tracks, approximately a mile south of Ezra Church and just beyond Utoy Creek.

General Hood, however, knew the Northern army's goal. He received regular intelligence from his cavalry, which diligently tracked the Union troops' movements. Hood ordered another division to reinforce Lee's troops, stretching the line of soldiers from the main Confederate perimeter to the South Fork of Utoy Creek. The Southern forces then built rifle pits and artillery bastions that reached a mile or more below

East Point.

On August 4th, Sherman decided that the time had come to seize the railroad. He ordered his soldiers not to stop until they had control of it. The first fight between the Union and Confederate soldiers led to 83 Northern soldiers killed and 140 captured Southern soldiers. Unperturbed by the modest advance, the Army of the Ohio, supported by one corps from the Army of the Cumberland, started crossing Utoy Creek.

The next day, the Union soldiers had to halt for the army to regroup. This pause, while necessary, allowed the Confederate forces to reinforce their defenses. The Southern troops went the extra mile by felling trees and using them to build an abatis.

When the Northern troops charged to fight, the Southern army responded with a tempest of musket and cannon fire. The charge was repulsed, and the Confederates got the upper hand. Seventy-six Union soldiers were killed, 199 were wounded, and 31 were captured, compared to 15 to 20 casualties on the Confederate side. That was over three hundred casualties for the Union forces and a maximum of twenty for the Confederates.

Undaunted, Sherman kept adjusting his strategy so his men could cut off the railroad. Despite the Union men's unwavering courage, the Northern assault faltered. The Confederate soldiers, though outnumbered, stood resolute. Their defenses proved impregnable. The Union soldiers couldn't breach them unassisted. Even when reinforcements came, their valorous effort led to almost two hundred casualties.

By the time the Battle of Utoy Creek was over, the Union losses ranged from between close to one thousand and as many as two thousand soldiers killed, wounded, captured, or missing. The South, on the other hand, lost about 250.

The Battle of Utoy Creek, in terms of casualties, might not have been a major engagement. But its importance lay in its strategic implication. The South had successfully thwarted the North's attempt to sever a critical supply line into Atlanta. The victory convinced General Sherman that infantry assaults against obstacles and trenches were futile. These frontal assaults on Confederate soldiers were not the path to victory. As the dust of the battle settled, Sherman's armies settled into their encirclement of Atlanta, besieging the city with more determination.

The Confederates kept guarding the railroad. They had won the battle and hoped to continue winning. Their victory bolstered them, and soon, the Southern army decided to launch a counterattack.

Desperate to break the siege, General Hood sent a Confederate cavalry commander, Major General Joseph Wheeler, on a daring raid. He decided to go to northern Georgia to cut Sherman's supply lines and destroy railroad tracks, which would halt the Union Army's relentless advance to Atlanta. On August 14th, Confederate forces closed in on a Union garrison at Dalton, Georgia, commanded by Colonel Bernard Leybold. They demanded the surrender of the garrison, but the Union commander refused to yield.

Outnumbered and facing insurmountable odds, the Union garrison retreated to fortifications atop a hill outside the town's boundaries. The two cavalries sporadically fought through the night, their gunfire punctuating the darkness like angry fireflies.

As dawn broke on the horizon, the Confederate raiders renewed their onslaught, but Leybold's men held firm. When all seemed lost for the Northern garrison, reinforcements from Chattanooga arrived. A four-hour skirmish ensued. By the end of the clash, Wheeler's cavalry reluctantly withdrew from the battlefield. The extent of the Confederates' damage to the railroad track is debatable. However, repairs began almost immediately. Within two days, trains rode along those rails. This skirmish came to be known as the Second Battle of Dalton.

There is also no record of the number of casualties in the battle. Although it was inconclusive by traditional measures, the Second Battle of Dalton could be counted as a Union victory. The Confederates had chosen to withdraw and had been unable to completely cut off the Union Army's supplies.

With Wheeler's cavalry absent, General Sherman set out to cripple General Hood's supply lines. He sent Union Brigadier General Judson Kilpatrick on that mission. On August 18th, 1864, Kilpatrick's cavalry arrived at the Atlanta and West Point Railroad. Tools clutched in determined hands, they destroyed parts of the railroad tracks with fervor. The metallic screech of twisted steel echoed in the air. They burned the Confederate supplies at the Jonesborough depot the next day. The precious Southern army supplies that had been piled high sent plumes of smoke billowing into the sky.

The Union forces continued their destruction at Lovejoy's Station on August 20th but were interrupted by Confederate forces, who fought with them into the night. Eventually, Kilpatrick was forced to flee to avoid being encircled by the enemy troops.

The Union and Confederate casualties were almost equal—almost 240 men on each side. But the battle was a Confederate victory since the Union soldiers withdrew. The Southern forces had thwarted the Northern troops. They prevented further destruction to the railroad and ensured it was in good working condition two days later.

General Sherman needed a decisive victory, and time was no longer on his side. The presidential election was in November. If he didn't capture Atlanta, President Abraham Lincoln could possibly not be reelected. On August 25th, Sherman ordered six divisions to march south of the city. Their destination was the Macon and Western Railroad, nestled near Jonesborough, Georgia.

General Hood thought it was business as usual. Unaware of the large number of the Northern troops, he discharged two corps to disrupt their advance. On August 31st, the Confederate forces launched a ferocious assault on two Union corps. However, the Federal soldiers were not easily swayed. They stood their ground and forced the Southern troops to retreat.

With a sinking heart, Hood realized the enormity of the Union presence gathering south of Atlanta. Since his army was vastly outnumbered, he had to make an agonizing decision: focus on the battle at Jonesborough or strongly defend Atlanta. Fearing a Union assault, Hood ordered one of the Confederate corps to return to defend the city.

Meanwhile, Sherman's forces relentlessly fought at Jonesborough. The Union soldiers eventually won. Hood's corps had about 2,000 casualties, and the Union had 1,149.

Now that the Union had won the railroad, the soldiers set to the task that would doom the Confederates. They ripped and tore at the iron sinews of the Macon and Western Railroad. They made good work of it, destroying one rail after the other until they were drenched in sweat. Each rail wrenched was a victory for which they had fought long and hard. Each torn piece of the rail track was a sure sign of complete victory.

While the soldiers rendered the railroad unusable, they heard a distant whistle. Soon, a train from Atlanta hurtled toward them. Upon sighting the destroyed rail lines, the train came to an abrupt halt. To flee from the impending danger, it reversed its course and went back to Atlanta, taking with it the news that the Confederate supply line had been cut. The enormity of the Union triumph dawned on the soldiers when they saw the looks on the faces of those on the train. Meanwhile, a sense of defeat clawed into the Confederate forces when they realized that their supply line had been severed.

Hood faced a reality of doom. Sixty thousand Federal troops now massed on the southern part of Atlanta. His communication and supply lines were also severed, a problem that would prove devastating for the Confederates. Atlanta, once a mighty stronghold and symbol of Southern pride, now teetered on the precipice of surrender. There was only one choice left for General Hood and his Confederate Army—abandon the city they had fought so fiercely to defend.

Chapter 8 – The Fall of Atlanta

Whitehall Street, a business district in Atlanta in the 1860s before Union soldiers burned down.
No known restrictions; https://www.loc.gov/item/2018666987/

Atlanta's citizens experienced the grim battles from within the city. Young Carrie Berry had to endure the trauma of war at such a young age. Sherman's army had constantly been bombarding Atlanta since July.

When the Union and Confederate forces battled or were involved in skirmishes, the shells landing on the city increased, and Carrie had to hide out in their small cellar. And when the shelling wasn't as intense, they cleaned up the house, cooked, knitted, visited the scarce number of friends and relatives left in Atlanta, or went to church if possible.

While the Confederate raiders retreated on August 15th, the morning started like any other for Carrie. She was already used to the shells falling in her city and hoped that she would get some reprieve that day.

She'd just finished eating breakfast and left the dining room when a monstrous shell filled with steel balls landed with a sinister thud by the garden gate. It made a large hole in the ground, then burst with a roar as it scattered dirt all over the yard. Some fragments from the shell flew from the garden and fell into the dining room. Carrie went pale. With trembling limbs and a racing heart, she fled to the cellar, where she stayed until it was time for dinner. Unfortunately, the shells did not relent. The next day, a shell flew into her mother's room and fell on the bed. Luckily, they were in the cellar when the shell fragments burst; otherwise, they might not have lived to see another day.

The shells kept landing in the city and increasing in intensity. On August 20th, a shell passed through her uncle's house and burned it down. That prompted her family to move downtown for a while. They lived in the cellar of Jacob's store at Five Points, a district where five streets intersected.

By the time Sherman had focused on destroying the railroad, he moved most of his soldiers to face the Confederates. The Union forces abandoned their breastworks to march on where they would win the war against Atlanta. The shelling on the city reduced drastically, and Carrie's family moved back home on August 27th. Carrie even looked for her schoolteacher so she could resume school.

On September 1st, Carrie's cousin Emma told her family that the Confederates would leave Atlanta that evening and that the Union Army would occupy it the next day. That night, the Southern army set fire to its ammunition to prevent Northern soldiers from acquiring them and using the weapons against the South. The Confederate mill was burned and razed to the ground. Then, the soldiers broke into stores, trying to get all they could before leaving.

After the Confederates abandoned Atlanta and left, the Union troops marched into defenseless Atlanta on September 2nd, 1864. Two days later, Sherman declared the end of the Atlanta Campaign. His proclamation, which was Special Field Order No. 64, signaled that Atlanta was theirs. The city, once a symbol of defiance, now stood under a new banner.

But in mid-November, Sherman gave a devastating order. It was toward the end of fall when leaves turned orange, yellow, and brown, and the trees shed their leaves. Just like leaves that change color are dying, the general's order changed Atlanta for the worse.

Before he began his "March to the Sea," Sherman sent his soldiers to set fire to the city's munitions factories, railway yards, and clothing mills. The flames did not stop at burning military resources; they consumed everything in their path. The fire turned into a relentless inferno that left Atlanta in ruins.

Conclusion

The Battle of Atlanta was a defining moment in the American Civil War and in American history. It was filled with bravery, sacrifice, and untold human resilience. There were smoke-filled skies and blood-soaked fields. There were men and women, soldiers and civilians who fought for their beliefs, their homes, and their very existence.

Think about President Abraham Lincoln, who got reelected after Atlanta was defeated. Think about General Sherman and General Hood, as well as the Union and Confederate soldiers. Now, imagine Gussie's short life because she volunteered at the military hospitals and contracted typhoid. Her sister, Sarah Clayton, wrote a memoir years later about the dangers they encountered during the war, and Gussie's remains were interred at Oakland Cemetery.

How about Carrie Berry, whose trials didn't end with the Union Army taking over Atlanta? First, two Union soldiers took their hog and made a meal out of it in early November. Her relations, neighbors, and friends left the city. Then, on November 12th, the soldiers began to burn stores and houses. By November 16th, the whole town was on fire, and the Yankees left in the afternoon. Carrie and her family endured the smoke and inferno. Luckily, their house did not burn, and they went on to rebuild their lives in Atlanta.

The Battle of Atlanta had far-reaching effects. It was a pivotal event in the Civil War. For President Lincoln, the victory breathed life into his reelection campaign. But what is more important is how Atlanta handled the rampage and destruction.

The Civil War eventually ended on April 9th, 1865. The citizens of Atlanta, once ravaged by the flames of war, began to rebuild. In 1868, Atlanta became the capital of Georgia as a symbol of rebirth and renewal. In 1877, it became the permanent capital by popular vote. Today, there are no pre-Civil War buildings in the city. The scars of war will always mark Atlanta's history, but its spirit has remained unbroken as it has risen from the ashes of war.

Here's another book by Captivating History that you might like

Free Bonus from Captivating History (Available for a Limited time)

Hi History Lovers!

Now you have a chance to join our exclusive history list so you can get your first history ebook for free as well as discounts and a potential to get more history books for free! Simply visit the link below to join.

Captivatinghistory.com/ebook

Also, make sure to follow us on Facebook, Twitter and Youtube by searching for Captivating History.

References

Academic Accelerator. (n.d.). *Second battle of Dalton.* https://academic-accelerator.com/encyclopedia/second-battle-of-dalton

America's Library. (n.d.). *Atlanta's role in the civil war.* https://www.americaslibrary.gov/es/ga/es_ga_atlanta_1.html

American Battlefield Trust. (n.d.). *Battle of Ezra Church.* https://www.battlefields.org/learn/articles/battle-ezra-church

American Battlefield Trust. (n.d.). *Battle of Peach Tree Creek.* https://www.battlefields.org/learn/articles/battle-peach-tree-creek

American Battlefield Trust (n.d.). *Battle of Utoy Creek.* https://www.battlefields.org/learn/articles/battle-utoy-creek

American Battlefield Trust. (n.d.). *Fulton County, GA / Jul 20, 1864.* https://www.battlefields.org/learn/civil-war/battles/peach-tree-creek

Atlanta in the American Civil War. (2023, February 28). In *Wikipedia.* https://en.wikipedia.org/w/index.php?title=Atlanta_in_the_American_Civil_War&oldid=1142067860

Battle of Atlanta. (2023, May 24). In *Wikipedia.* https://en.wikipedia.org/w/index.php?title=Battle_of_Atlanta&oldid=1156674045

Berry, C. M. (1897). *Carrie Berry's diary.* Atlanta History Center. https://dlg.galileo.usg.edu/turningpoint/ahc/cw/pdfs/ahc0029f-001.pdf

Cutrer, T. W. (2018, March 29). *Hood, John Bell (1831-1879).* Texas State Historical Association. https://www.tshaonline.org/handbook/entries/hood-john-bell

Davis, S. (2018, September 17). *Atlanta campaign.* New Georgia Encyclopedia. https://www.georgiaencyclopedia.org/articles/history-archaeology/atlanta-campaign/

ExploreATL. (n.d.). *Battle of Atlanta: Civil War tipping point.* https://sites.google.com/exploreatl.com/battle-of-atlanta/

Gordy, J. (2019, February 20). *5 things to know about the Battle of Atlanta cyclorama.* Atlanta History Center. https://www.atlantahistorycenter.com/blog/5-things-to-know-about-the-battle-of-atlanta-cyclorama/

Greenwalt, P. (2014, August 31). *Jonesborough, Georgia: The battle that doomed Atlanta.* Emerging Civil War. https://emergingcivilwar.com/2014/08/31/jonesborough-georgia-the-battle-that-doomed-atlanta/

Haber, E. (2018, August 29). *Spotlight on the women of Atlanta during the Civil War.* Historic Oakland Foundation. https://oaklandcemetery.com/spotlight-on-the-women-of-atlanta-during-the-civil-war/

Harper's New Monthly Magazine. (1865, October). *Atlanta in ruins* [Illustration]. New Georgia Encyclopedia. https://www.georgiaencyclopedia.org/articles/history-archaeology/atlanta-campaign/

Hickman, K. (2017, March 6). *American Civil War: Battle of Ezra Church.* ThoughtCo. https://www.thoughtco.com/battle-of-ezra-church-2360231

Hudson, M. (2022, July 15). *Battle of Atlanta.* Encyclopedia Britannica. https://www.britannica.com/event/Battle-of-Atlanta

Library of Congress. (n.d.). *William T. Sherman.* https://www.loc.gov/exhibits/civil-war-in-america/biographies/william-t-sherman.html

Library of Congress. (1864). *Destruction of the depots, public buildings, and manufactories at Atlanta, Georgia, November 15. 1864. The fourteenth and twentieth corps moving out of Atlanta, November 15, 1864.* https://www.loc.gov/item/00652832/

McPherson, J. M. (Ed.). (1994). *The atlas of the Civil War.* Macmillan.

Monovisions Black & White Photography Magazine. (n.d.). *Vintage: Everyday life of Atlanta, Georgia (19th century).* https://monovisions.com/vintage-everyday-life-of-atlanta-georgia-19th-century/

N-Georgia. (n.d.). *The Civil War battle at Lovejoy Station.* https://www.n-georgia.com/lovejoy-station-civil-war-battle.html

N-Georgia. (n.d.). *The second Civil War battle in Dalton.* https://www.n-georgia.com/dalton-civil-war-battle2.html

National Geographic. (n.d.). *Apr 12, 1861 CE: Battle of Fort Sumter.* https://education.nationalgeographic.org/resource/battle-fort-sumter/

New York Historical Society Museum & Library. (n.d.). *Surviving the siege of Atlanta.* https://wams.nyhistory.org/a-nation-divided/civil-war/surviving-siege-of-atlanta/

Ohio Civil War Central. (n.d.). *Battle of Ezra Church.* https://www.ohiocivilwarcentral.com/battle-of-ezra-church/

Ohio Civil War Central. (n.d.). *Battle of Lovejoy's Station.* https://www.ohiocivilwarcentral.com/battle-of-lovejoys-station/

Ohio Civil War Central. (n.d.). *Battle of Utoy Creek.* https://www.ohiocivilwarcentral.com/battle-of-utoy-creek/

Onion, A., Sullivan, M., Mullen, M., ... Zapata, C. (2020, July 21). *Battle of Atlanta continues.* https://www.history.com/this-day-in-history/battle-of-atlanta-continues

Onion, A., Sullivan, M., Mullen, M., ... Zapata, C. (2020, August 31). *Atlanta falls to Union forces.* History. https://www.history.com/this-day-in-history/atlanta-falls-to-union-forces

Pollock, D. A. (2014, May 30). *The Battle of Atlanta: History and remembrance.* Southern Spaces. https://southernspaces.org/2014/battle-atlanta-history-and-remembrance/

Robertson, J. (2019, July 18). *John Bell Hood.* Radio IQ. https://www.wvtf.org/civil-war-series/2019-07-08/john-bell-hood

Searles, H. (2022, May 5). *Second battle of Dalton.* American History Central. https://www.americanhistorycentral.com/entries/second-battle-of-dalton/

Searles, H. (2022, May 6). *Battle of Jonesborough.* American History Central. https://www.americanhistorycentral.com/entries/jonesborough-battle-of/

Searles. H. (2023, April 29). *The Battle of Lovejoy's Station, 1864.* American History Central. https://www.americanhistorycentral.com/entries/battle-of-lovejoys-station/

Searles, H. (2023, August 10). *Battle of Utoy Creek facts.* American History Central. https://www.americanhistorycentral.com/entries/battle-of-utoy-creek-facts/

The Army Historical Foundation. (n.d.). *General William Tecumseh Sherman.* https://armyhistory.org/general-william-tecumseh-sherman/

The Editors of Encyclopedia Britannica. (2021, October 13). *Battle of Atlanta summary.* Encyclopedia Britannica. https://www.britannica.com/summary/Battle-of-Atlanta

The Editors of Encyclopedia Britannica. (2023, March 17). *Joseph E. Johnston.* Encyclopedia Britannica.

https://www.britannica.com/biography/Joseph-E-Johnston

The Ohio State University. (n.d.). *John Bell Hood.* https://ehistory.osu.edu/biographies/john-bell-hood

The Ohio State University. (n.d.). *Ezra church (Battle of the poor house).* https://ehistory.osu.edu/battles/ezra-church-battle-poor-house

United States Senate. (n.d.). *Civil War begins.* https://www.senate.gov/artandhistory/history/minute/Civil_War_Begins.htm

Made in the USA
Las Vegas, NV
19 December 2023